The Healthy Puppy

Cookbook

Homemade Healthy Treats for Your Dog

BY: Alicia T. White

License Note!

I know you've read this and seen this in many other books and movies. Still, there's a reason why authors and filmmakers are so adamant about protecting their copyrights despite it being so annoying for you to see yet again… The thing is, lots of people infringe on copyrights, and this greatly affects our work negatively.

Thus, here we go again just so things are clear:

Do not make any print or electronic reproductions, sell, re-publish, or distribute this book in parts or as a whole unless you have express written consent from me or my team.

I spent over 4 months working on this cookbook, so I protect it like it's my baby! I know you can understand the value of working hard on something and wanting to protect your end product, so please help me by not infringing on the copyright or letting others do so.

Thanks!

Table of Contents

Introduction:

Dogs are frequently referred to as man's best friend.

Because they have always been there for us throughout history.

We must now be there for them.

According to studies, over processed dog food is bad for your dog's health, which is where this book comes in.

You'll find tons of recipes that your dog will love on these pages.

These homemade meals and treats will not only get your dog excited about mealtime, but they will also help to ensure that your dog isn't eating harmful chemicals with every meal.

OOOOOOOOOOOOOOOOOOOOOOOOOOOOOOOOOOOOOOOO

Chicken Recipes

OOOOOOOOOOOOOOOOOOOOOOOOOOOOOOOOOOOOOO

1. Pumpkin Puree Chicken Meal

Preparation Time:10min

Cooking Time:50min

Total Prep Time:1h

Makes:1-2

Ingredient List:

- 2 boneless and skinless chicken breasts, bite-size pieces
- ½ cup cooked brown rice
- ½ cup of green peas
- ½ cup dehydrated food
- 1 diced apple
- ½ cup diced carrots
- 1 potato, bite-size pieces
- 1 cup of pumpkin puree
- ¼ cup of water

OOOOOOOOOOOOOOOOOOOOOOOOOOOOOOOOOOOOOOO

Procedure:

1. Preheat the oven to 325°F.
2. Place the chicken pieces in a saucepan and cover with water. Set over medium-high heat, and once boiling, lower the heat and let it simmer for 30 minutes.
3. In another saucepan, boil the potato for 30 minutes.
4. Cook the rice separately.
5. Once everything is ready, transfer it into a large bowl. Add the remaining ingredients and stir well.
6. Spoon into a large casserole dish.
7. Bake for about 20 minutes.
8. Let it cool down, and serve. Keep the leftovers in the fridge.

2. Chicken Veggie Mix

Preparation Time:10min

Cooking Time:2h

Total Prep Time:2h 10min

Makes:10-16

Ingredient List:

- 3 pounds chicken breasts and thighs, skinless and boneless
- 2 tablespoons oil
- 1 apple (large) cubed and removed the seeds
- 2 carrots, cut into pieces
- 1 cubed sweet potato
- 2 cups peas, frozen
- 2 cups green beans, frozen
- 1 can (15 ounces) kidney beans, rinsed
- 4 cups of water

OOOOOOOOOOOOOOOOOOOOOOOOOOOOOOOOOOOOOOO

Procedure:

1. Add the chicken to a stock pot and pour in the water.
2. Add the apple, green beans, kidney beans, carrots, and potato.
3. Cook for 2 hours on low heat. To prevent sticking, stir frequently and add water as needed.
4. Once the liquid has been drained.
5. Pour the oil in.
6. Consistently mash and stir.
7. When completely cool, divide into single servings and place in the freezer. Always defrost food in the fridge overnight.

3. Chicken Spinach and Apple Dinner

Preparation Time:20min

Cooking Time:40min

Total Prep Time:1h

Makes:16-20

Ingredient List:

- 5 pounds chicken (use the whole chicken including the livers, heart, and neck meat)
- 2 apples, peeled and diced
- 2 cups red cabbage, chopped
- 2 cups spinach, chopped
- 5 eggs, cooked
- 2 tablespoons oil

OOOOOOOOOOOOOOOOOOOOOOOOOOOOOOOOOOOOOOOO

Procedure:

1. Remove the meat from the bones and chop it.
2. Transfer it to a pot and bring it to a boil for about 30 minutes.
3. Cook on medium-high heat.
4. Reduce the temperature to medium and add the apples, spinach, and cabbage.
5. Cook for 10 minutes. Set it aside and let it cool.
6. Combine the oil and eggs. Constantly stir.
7. Serve and freeze leftovers in single portions.

4. *Chicken Liver and Turkey Meal*

Preparation Time:15min

Cooking Time:20min

Total Prep Time:35min

Makes:6-10

Ingredient List:

- 2 pounds of ground turkey
- 2 tablespoons of chicken liver, pureed or diced
- 2 tablespoons of safflower oil
- 1 cup of broccoli florets
- 2 carrots, chopped
- ½ zucchini, chopped
- 1 cup cauliflower florets

OOOOOOOOOOOOOOOOOOOOOOOOOOOOOOOOOOOOOO

Procedure:

1. First, steam the carrots for 10 minutes.
2. Meanwhile, cook the liver and turkey over medium-high heat in a skillet.
3. Cook for 15 minutes. Discard the fat and set it aside.
4. Add the zucchini, cauliflower, and broccoli to the steamer and continue to steam for 8 more minutes.
5. In a large container, combine all ingredients.
6. Drizzle with the safflower oil and toss.
7. Let it cool before serving and freezing.

5. Chicken with Rolled Oats

Preparation Time: 10min

Cooking Time: 10min

Total Prep Time: 20 min

Makes: 8 cups

Ingredient List:

- 3 pounds chicken breasts, skinless and boneless
- 3 cups of rolled oats, cooked (old-fashioned)
- 1 cup carrots, shredded
- 2 cups yellow squash, shredded
- 1 cup green peas, frozen, thawed
- ½ cup parsley, chopped

OOOOOOOOOOOOOOOOOOOOOOOOOOOOOOOOOOOOOOOO

Procedure:

1. Place the chicken breasts in a saucepan and add water to cover the meat.
2. Once boiling, lower the heat to medium and let it simmer for 10 minutes. Set aside and let it cool down in the saucepan for about 30 minutes.
3. Cut the chicken into pieces and set aside the broth.
4. Combine the parsley, peas, shredded veggies, and oats in a mixing bowl.
5. Add the chicken broth, half a cup, until you reach the consistency your dog likes.
6. Serve and store in the fridge for 3 days or in the freezer for 3 weeks.

6. Chicken Healthy Salad

Preparation Time:10min

Cooking Time:25

Total Prep Time:35min

Makes:4-8

ingredient list:

- 1 pound chicken
- 2 zucchini, sliced
- 3 cups green beans
- 3 cups kale, chopped
- 1 cup quinoa

OOOOOOOOOOOOOOOOOOOOOOOOOOOOOOOOOOOOOO

Procedure:

1. In a pot, add 2 cups of water. Add the quinoa and boil for 15 minutes.
2. In the meantime, slice the chicken.
3. Drizzle with oil and place in a skillet.
4. Turn the heat up to medium-high. Cook for 15 minutes.
5. Add the veggies and cook for 10 more minutes.
6. Stir in the cooked quinoa.
7. Let it cool and serve.

7. Chicken Casserole

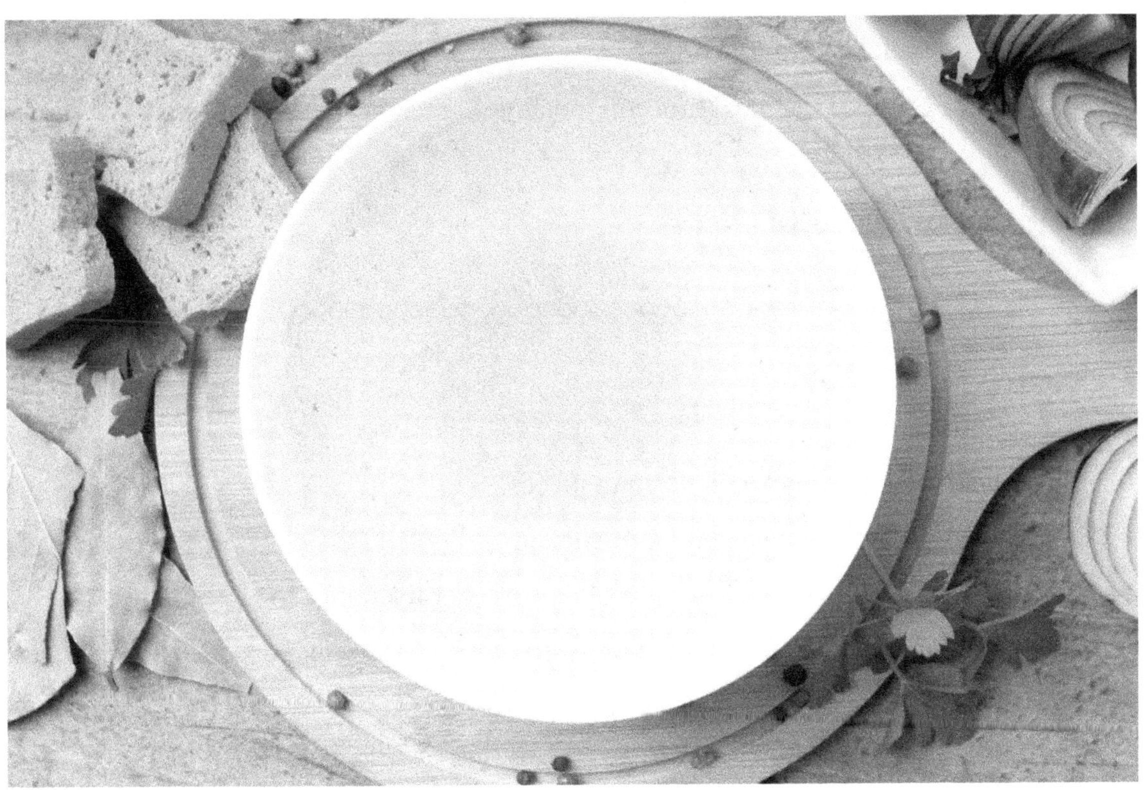

Preparation Time:10min

Cooking Time:25

Total Prep Time:30min

Makes:8-12

Ingredient List:

- 2 pounds skinless and boneless chicken breasts
- 2 cups of chicken broth
- 1 cup of chopped veggies (broccoli, potatoes, green beans, carrots, etc.)
- Oil
- 1/4 cup of rolled oats

OOOOOOOOOOOOOOOOOOOOOOOOOOOOOOOOOOOOOOOO

Procedure:

1. To begin, cut the chicken into small pieces.
2. Sauté in oil for 15 minutes or until cooked.
3. Next, add the broth, veggies, and rolled oats. Let it simmer for 15 minutes.
4. Once cooled, serve and store the leftovers in single-serving portions in the freezer.

Beef Recipes

8. Beef Liver Meal

Preparation Time:30min

Cooking Time:2h

Total Prep Time:2h 30min

Makes:30-42

Ingredient List:

- 1 pound of beef liver
- 5 pounds of beef roast
- 5 cups of mixed vegetables
- 1 cup of brown rice

ooooooooooooooooooooooooooooooooooooooo

Procedure:

1. Roast the beef for 1 hour and 30 minutes, or until the internal temperature reaches 170°F.
2. Allow it to rest for a few minutes before cutting it into pieces.
3. Fry the liver for a few minutes or until medium rare.
4. Dice the veggies into cubes. Blanch them for about 1 minute.
5. Bring a pot of water to a boil.
6. Cook for about 25 minutes after adding the rice, or follow the instructions on the package.
7. In a large mixing bowl, combine and stir everything together.
8. Serve and store leftovers in the freezer.

9. Classic Beef Meal

Preparation Time:10min

Cooking Time:30min

Total Prep Time:40min

Makes:6

Ingredient List:

- 1 shredded zucchini
- ½ cup frozen or canned peas
- 3 cups chopped baby spinach
- 2 shredded carrots
- 1 tablespoon oil
- 3 pounds of ground turkey
- 1 ½ cups of brown rice

OOOOOOOOOOOOOOOOOOOOOOOOOOOOOOOOOOOOOO

Procedure:

1. First, cook the brown rice according to the package directions.
2. Set aside once completed.
3. Place a stockpot over medium heat.
4. Add 1 tablespoon of oil to the heat.
5. Cook for 5 minutes after adding the meat.
6. Cook for 5 minutes more after adding the remaining ingredients.
7. Set aside to cool. Serve and freeze the leftovers.

Preparation Time:15min

Cooking Time:30min

Total Prep Time:45min

Makes:4-6

Ingredient List:

- 1 pound of beef meat for stew
- ½ cup of chopped carrots
- 1 sweet potato, small
- 1 potato, small
- ½ cup flour
- ½ cup of water
- 1 tablespoon olive oil

OOOOOOOOOOOOOOOOOOOOOOOOOOOOOOOOOOOOOOOO

Procedure:

1. Peel the two kinds of potatoes.
2. Cut into small pieces.
3. Bake them for 10 minutes.
4. Meanwhile, cook the stew meat until it is done. Set aside.
5. Add water to the drippings first, then gradually add the flour.
6. Stir until it becomes thick.
7. Combine the potatoes, carrots, and beef in a large mixing bowl.
8. Cook for 10 minutes.
9. Serve cold.

11. Beef Vegetable Mix

Preparation Time:10min

Cooking Time:2 hours

Total Prep Time:2h 10min

Makes:6

Ingredient List:

- ½ cup of canned or frozen peas
- 1 ½ cups of carrots, chopped
- 1 ½ cups of butternut squash, chopped
- 1 can of kidney beans (15 ounces) rinsed
- 1 ½ cups of brown rice
- 2 ½ pounds of ground beef
- 6 cups of water

OOOOOOOOOOOOOOOOOOOOOOOOOOOOOOOOOOOOOOO

Procedure:

1. Combine all the ingredients in a stockpot.
2. Cover the stockpot and place it over medium-high heat. Once boiling, lower the heat to low and let it cook for 2 hours.
3. If necessary, add water and stir frequently.
4. Once cooled, divide the leftovers into servings and freeze them later.

12. Lovely Meatballs

Preparation Time: 10min

Cooking Time: 30min

Total Prep Time: 40min

Makes: 6

Ingredient List:

- 1 pound ground beef
- ½ cup grated apples, raw
- 1 tablespoon parsley flakes
- 2 tablespoons omega 3 and 6 oil
- ¼ cup honey

OOOOOOOOOOOOOOOOOOOOOOOOOOOOOOOOOOOOOOOO

Procedure:

1. In a mixing bowl, combine all the ingredients and stir until well combined.
2. Dry them in olive oil or bake them in a pan or a muffin tray.
3. Once cool, serve and store leftovers in the refrigerator for 3 days or in the freezer.

13. Delicious Meatloaf

Preparation Time: 15min

Cooking Time: 40min

Total Prep Time: 55min

Makes: 4 -6

Ingredient List:

- ½ cup of cottage cheese
- 1 ½ cups of mixed veggies and fruits (apples, carrots, broccoli, or any other fruit that your dog enjoys)
- 1 ½ cups of rolled oats
- 2 eggs
- 1 pound ground beef

OOOOOOOOOOOOOOOOOOOOOOOOOOOOOOOOOOOOOOOOO

Procedure:

1. Preheat the oven to 350°F.
2. Grated the vegetables.
3. In a bowl, combine all ingredients and mix by hand until blended.
4. Transfer to a baking dish and bake for 40 minutes.
5. Let it cool and serve. Refrigerate for 3 days or freeze divided into servings for easier serving.

14. Chili Treats

Preparation Time: 10min

Cooking Time: 50min

Total Prep Time: 1h

Makes: 6

Ingredient List:

- 1 package macaroni
- 1 can (15 ounces) corn
- 2 cups of beef broth without salt
- 1 can (15 ounces) tomato paste
- 1 pound of ground beef
- 2 tablespoons of unsalted butter
- 4 carrots
- 1 tablespoon of oil

OOOOOOOOOOOOOOOOOOOOOOOOOOOOOOOOOOOOOOOO

Procedure:

1. Boil the macaroni according to package instructions.
2. Heat the oil in a pan over medium-high heat. Cook the ground beef for 5 minutes.
3. Add the tomato paste, corn, carrots, and butter. Cook for 5 more minutes.
4. In a casserole dish, combine the macaroni and the beef mixture. Add 2 cups of beef broth.
5. Bake for 30 minutes at 350°F.
6. Serve cool, and store the leftovers in the freezer.

Dog Treat Recipes

OOOOOOOOOOOOOOOOOOOOOOOOOOOOOOOOOOOOOO

15. Cheesy Treat

Preparation Time: 15min

Cooking Time: 3h

Total Prep Time: 3h 15min

Makes: 30-40

Ingredient List:

- 4 cups flour
- 2 tablespoons oil
- 2 cups cheese, shredded
- 1 1/3 cups water

OOOOOOOOOOOOOOOOOOOOOOOOOOOOOOOOOOOOOOOO

Procedure:

1. Combine the cheese and flour in a mixing bowl.
2. Pour in the water and oil.
3. If necessary, add more water to form a stiff dough.
4. Roll out the dough to a thickness of 3/8 inch and cut it into shapes.
5. Place on a cookie sheet and bake for 2 ½ to 3 hours at 250°F or until dry.
6. Allow it to cool on a rack before serving.

16. Almond Banana Treats

Preparation Time:20min

Cooking Time:10min

Total Prep Time:30min

Makes:10-15

Ingredient List:

- 1 egg
- 1/3 banana
- ¾ cup almond butter, unsalted
- 1 teaspoon cinnamon, ground

OOOOOOOOOOOOOOOOOOOOOOOOOOOOOOOOOOOOOOO

Procedure:

1. Preheat oven to 350°F.
2. Using parchment paper, line a baking dish.
3. Mash the banana in a mixing bowl, then add the remaining ingredients.
4. Combine thoroughly.
5. The batter should be thick and gooey.
6. Place in the oven after spooning into the baking dish.
7. Bake for 5 minutes. Turn the baking pan and bake for 5 more minutes.
8. Allow it to cool before serving. You can store it for 5 days.

17. Dog Biscuits

Preparation Time:20min

Cooking Time:30min

Total Prep Time:50min

Makes:15-20

Ingredient List:

- ½ cup beef stock
- 2 ½ cups oat flour or wheat flour
- ½ cup dehydrated chicken, cheese, or bacon pieces
- 1 egg

OOOOOOOOOOOOOOOOOOOOOOOOOOOOOOOOOOOOOOOOOOO

Procedure:

1. Preheat the oven to 350°F.
2. Combine the bacon bits, egg, beef stock, and flour in a bowl.
3. Make the dough and roll it out to a thickness of ½ inch.
4. Cut into desired shapes and place on a baking sheet lined with parchment paper.
5. Bake for 25-30 minutes in the oven
6. Allow them to cool on a rack before giving them to your dog.

18. Fruit Desserts

Preparation Time:5min

Cooking Time:/

Total Prep Time:5min

Makes:1

Ingredient List:

- ¼ cup of applesauce
- ½ cup of blueberries
- ¼ cup of yogurt
- ¼ cup of strawberries
- ¼ cup apples, diced
- optional – 1 tablespoon of brewer's yeast

OOOOOOOOOOOOOOOOOOOOOOOOOOOOOOOOOOOOOOOO

Procedure:

1. Combine all the ingredients in a blender.
2. Blend until you get a smooth texture.
3. Serve.

19. Pumpkin Bites

Preparation Time:20min

Cooking Time:30min

Total Prep Time:50min

Makes:15

Ingredient List:

- 1 cup wheat flour
- ¼ cup carrots, shredded
- 1 egg, beaten slightly
- ¾ cup of canned pumpkin (purchase one with only pumpkin inside)

OOOOOOOOOOOOOOOOOOOOOOOOOOOOOOOOOOOOOOOO

Procedure:

1. First, preheat the oven to 350°F.
2. In a bowl, combine all ingredients. Mix well to make the dough.
3. Roll the dough into balls and then place them on a baking sheet lined with parchment paper.
4. Bake for about 30 minutes.
5. Let it cool and serve.

20. Meatloaf for a Delicious Treat

Preparation Time: 15min

Cooking Time: 30min

Total Prep Time: 45 min

Makes: 10

Ingredient List:

- 3 cups of your dog's favorite ground meat (beef, turkey, or chicken)
- 2 eggs
- ½ cup of cottage cheese
- ½ cup grated veggies
- ½ cup of rolled oats

OOOOOOOOOOOOOOOOOOOOOOOOOOOOOOOOOOOOOOOO

Procedure:

1. Preheat the oven to 350°F.
2. In a bowl, mix all ingredients and mix well. Form balls and place them on a baking dish lined with parchment paper.
3. Bake for 30 minutes until well cooked
4. Serve as a treat or snack.

21. Veggie Smoothie

Preparation Time:5min

Cooking Time:/

Total Prep Time:5min

Makes:1

Ingredient List:

- ¼ cup of this mix: collards, spinach, green beans, zucchini, squash, and carrots
- ¼ cup mix of bananas, pears, peaches, and apples
- ¼ cup any fruit juice (not grape juice)
- 1 tablespoon of cream cheese
- 4 tablespoons of yogurt

OOOOOOOOOOOOOOOOOOOOOOOOOOOOOOOOOOOOOO

Procedure:

1. In a blender, combine all of the ingredients.
2. Blend until completely smooth.
3. Serve right away.

Cooking with Fish

OOOOOOOOOOOOOOOOOOOOOOOOOOOOOOOOOOOOOOOO

22. Broccoli Fish Fillet Recipe

Preparation Time:5min

Cooking Time:15min

Total Prep Time:20min

Makes:4

Ingredient List:

- 1 pound fish fillets, cut into small pieces
- ½ cup broccoli florets
- ½ cup chopped carrots
- ½ cup cauliflower
- 1 tablespoon oil
- 1 cup kale

OOOOOOOOOOOOOOOOOOOOOOOOOOOOOOOOOOOOOO

Procedure:

1. Turn the heat to medium.
2. Place the carrots, broccoli, and cauliflower in a skillet.
3. Cook for 10 minutes, or until the water evaporates, after adding 1/2 cup of water.
4. Add the fish and the oil.
5. Cook for 2 minutes before adding the Kale.
6. Continue to cook for another 2 minutes.
7. Allow it to cool before serving.
8. Keep any leftovers in the refrigerator.

23. Salmon Spinach Scramble

Preparation Time: 5min

Cooking Time: 7min

Total Prep Time: 12min

Makes: 1

Ingredient List:

- 1 teaspoon oil
- ½ a can of salmon, boneless and skinless, drained
- 2 eggs
- ½ cup spinach, frozen, thawed

ooooooooooooooooooooooooooooooooooooo

Procedure:

1. Place a skillet over medium heat.
2. Drizzle in the oil and heat.
3. Mix in the salmon and spinach.
4. Cook for 5 minutes.
5. Continue to cook for 2 minutes after cracking in 2 eggs.
6. Allow it to cool before serving.

24. Super Easy Mixed Fish Dinner

Preparation Time:10min

Cooking Time:10min

Total Prep Time:20min

Makes:6

Ingredient List:

- 2 pounds fish fillets (swai and tilapia are excellent choices, and frozen is also acceptable.)
- 1-2 cans of pink salmon
- 3 eggs, cooked
- 3 cups veggies (a combination of kale, green beans, and cabbage or anything else your dog prefers)
- 1 cup cooked lentils

OOOOOOOOOOOOOOOOOOOOOOOOOOOOOOOOOOOOOO

Procedure:

1. Cook the mixed vegetables for 5 minutes over medium-high heat.
2. Place the grain in a bowl.
3. Cook the fish fillets for 2 minutes in a skillet, constantly stirring on medium-high heat.
4. Place in the bowl with the vegetables.
5. Add the remaining ingredients and mix well.
6. Let it cool completely before serving. Store the leftovers in the fridge for 3 days. You can also freeze it.

25. Salmon Patties

Preparation Time:10min

Cooking Time:20min

Total Prep Time:30min

Makes:1

Ingredient List:

- 1 egg
- 1 can of salmon
- 1 carrot
- 1 celery
- 1 potato
- 1 tablespoon oil
- 3 tablespoons flour

OOOOOOOOOOOOOOOOOOOOOOOOOOOOOOOOOOOOOOOO

Procedure:

1. Chop the carrot, celery, and potatoes into small pieces.
2. Place the salmon in a bowl and pat it dry.
3. Mix in the egg and flour. Combine thoroughly.
4. Form the mixture into patties.
5. Cook for 6 minutes, stirring occasionally.
6. Stir-fry the veggies for 15 minutes.

Turkey Recipes

26. Turkey Stew

Preparation Time:10min

Cooking Time:1h 10min

Total Prep Time:1 h 20min

Makes:10

Ingredient List:

- 3 pounds turkey legs, boneless and skinless
- 1 cup of brown rice
- 1 can (15 ounces) of kidney beans
- 1 ½ cups carrots, chopped
- ⅓ cup peas
- 1 ½ cups butternut squash, chopped
- 1 cup broccoli florets
- 1 cup cauliflower florets
- 6 cups of water

OOOOOOOOOOOOOOOOOOOOOOOOOOOOOOOOOOOOOOOOO

Procedure:

1. Add the meat, rice, kidney beans, carrots, and squash to a pot.
2. Turn on the high heat and pour in the water.
3. Once the water is boiling, reduce the heat to medium and cover the pot.
4. Allow it to cook for 1 hour. If necessary, add more water.
5. After 1 hour, add the cauliflower, broccoli, and peas.
6. Place the meat on a plate and shred it.
7. Return to the pot. Let it simmer for 10 more minutes and set aside.
8. Let it cool and serve.
9. Store the leftovers in the freeze in single servings.

27. Classic Turkey Dish for Dogs

Preparation Time: 10min

Cooking Time: 10min

Total Prep Time: 20min

Makes: 10

Ingredient List:

- 1 ½ cups cooked brown rice
- 1 tablespoon oil
- 2 shredded carrots
- 1 shredded zucchini
- ½ cup of frozen peas
- 3 cups of spinach and kale mix, chopped
- 3 pounds of ground turkey

OOOOOOOOOOOOOOOOOOOOOOOOOOOOOOOOOOOOOOOO

Procedure:

1. Heat the oil in a stockpot over medium heat.
2. Cook the meat for 5 minutes. Crumble while you cook.
3. Add the brown rice, peas, zucchini, carrots, and green mix.
4. Cook for 5 minutes more and set aside.
5. Allow it to cool before serving.
6. Save the leftovers in a single meal in the freezer.

28. Baked Dish

Preparation Time:10min

Cooking Time:45min+

Total Prep Time:55min

Makes:40

Ingredient List:

- 7 pounds of ground turkey
- 3 pounds of ground beef
- 10 eggs, raw
- 5 cups brown rice, cooked
- 3 cups veggie mix

OOOOOOOOOOOOOOOOOOOOOOOOOOOOOOOOOOOOOOOO

Procedure:

1. Mix all of the ingredients in a mixing bowl and thoroughly combine.
2. Place on a baking sheet and roll into balls.
3. Bake each batch for 45 minutes at 400°F.
4. Once cooled, serve immediately or freeze in single batches.

29. Simple Turkey Rice

Preparation Time: 10min

Cooking Time: 12min

Total Prep Time: 22min

Makes: 4

Ingredient List:

- 1 pound ground turkey
- ½ cup shredded carrot
- ½ cup shredded zucchini
- 2 tablespoons spinach, chopped
- ½ cup shredded yellow squash
- 1 cup cooked brown rice
- 1 tablespoon oil

OOOOOOOOOOOOOOOOOOOOOOOOOOOOOOOOOOOOOOOO

Procedure:

1. Prepare the vegetables.
2. Melt the butter in a skillet over medium-high heat.
3. Add the ground turkey and the oil.
4. Cook for 5 minutes before adding the vegetables (except the spinach and rice).
5. Continue to cook for 5 minutes more.
6. Cook for 2 minutes after adding the spinach and rice.
7. Place aside.
8. Let it cool and serve. Keep the leftovers in the fridge.

30. Turkey Liver Mix

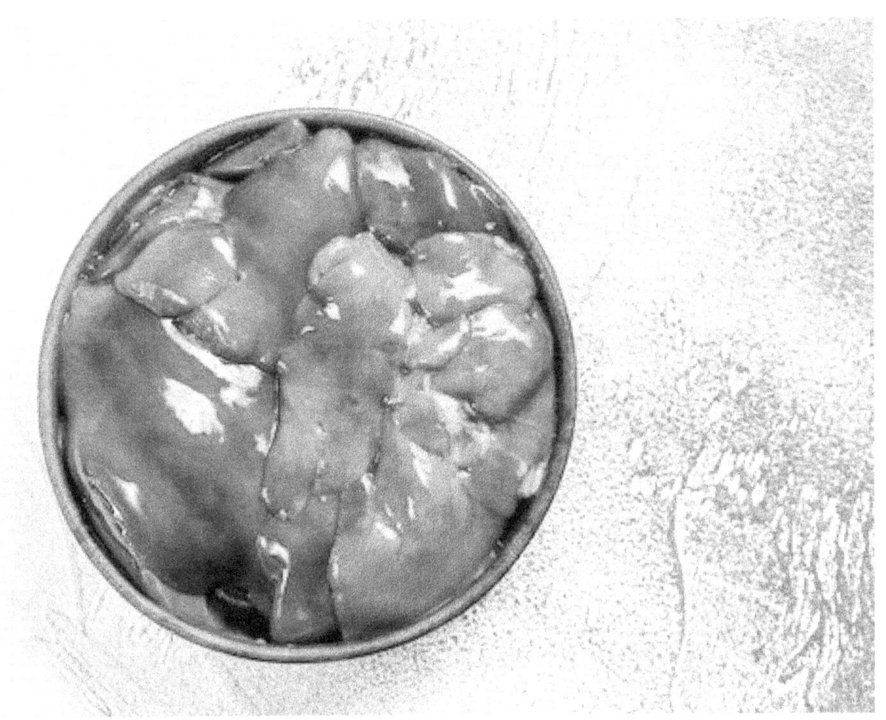

Preparation Time:15min

Cooking Time:40min

Total Prep Time:55min

Makes:10

Ingredient List:

- 2 pounds of ground turkey
- 3 tablespoons turkey liver, chopped
- ½ cup broccoli florets
- ½ cup cauliflower
- ½ sliced zucchini
- 2 carrots chopped
- 1 sweet potato, chopped and peeled
- 2 tablespoons oil

OOOOOOOOOOOOOOOOOOOOOOOOOOOOOOOOOOOOOOO

Procedure:

1. In a pot, add the sweet potato and carrots.
2. Cook for 10 minutes, and add the zucchini, cauliflower, and broccoli.
3. Cook for 10 more minutes. Drain and set aside in a bowl.
4. Add 1 tablespoon of oil to a skillet and cook the liver for 10 minutes over medium-high.
5. Set aside in the same bowl with the veggies.
6. Add the ground turkey and cook for 10 minutes, until well cooked.
7. Transfer to the bowl.
8. Add 1 tablespoon oil to the bowl and toss to combine.
9. Let it cool and serve. Freeze the leftover in single-serving packages.

Author's Note

Not many people do this, but I grew up under difficult circumstances where nothing was handed to me, and the only way forward was with your best effort. At some point, people started recognizing me for my talent in the kitchen despite my young age, and I've only worked harder from there!

Because I am constantly trying to improve my work, I would really appreciate your help. Sure, I always ask my friends and family for their feedback on my newest projects but, whether they want to accept it or not, there's always some sort of bias because they don't want to hurt my feelings by criticizing my work. Thus, I need a neutral pair of eyes — that's where you come in!

If you're up for it, I would appreciate you telling me what you think of my cookbooks. Are the recipes easy to follow? Did you get stuck somewhere? Are the measurements laid out? Any suggestions you may have are welcome. After all, cookbooks are only helpful when you actually understand them! Incorporating your ideas and suggestions into my new projects will be my show of eternal gratitude because you can only be the best at something by constantly improving and being open to change.

Thanks!

Alicia T. White

About the Author

Alicia had a tough childhood and had to take care of her siblings early. Although they often helped her with making the beds and washing, Alicia was responsible for cooking since she was the oldest of six. Being in the kitchen was still very difficult at her age, but she learned her way around the stove and oven throughout the years.

Whereas her first dishes were practically inedible, burnt rice and mushy pasta… Eventually, she turned to the oven for help as many of the dishes she wanted to make were too complicated. Nonetheless, her baked casseroles were amazing! Most importantly, they were simple and required way less clean-up.

At first, they were simple pasta bakes, but once Alicia got the hang of things, she was baking all sorts of meals. When it came to spreading the word of her delicious cooking, having 5 siblings was extremely advantageous. Soon, neighbors were placing orders for some of her casseroles! Eventually, Alicia was doing so well with the business that she hired extra help. Now it's one of the most affordable yet popular weeknight casserole services in the mid-West!

Today, she still lives with her siblings and is working hard to teach them about the family business that led them out of poverty. She likes to publish cookbooks on casseroles and one-pot meals in her free time— basically anything quick and easy. Her motto is, "If a seven-year-old can't make it, it isn't simple enough!"